THE
PATTERN
OF LANDSCAPE

Applied Ecology, Landscape and Natural Resource Management Series

W.M. Adams (ed), *Conservation and Agriculture — the Debate 1981-1984*

W.M. Adams & J. Budd (eds), *Monitoring Countryside Change*

G. Dawe, *Habitat Creation*

B. Hackett, *Landscape Conservation*

D.R. Helliwell, *Economics of Woodland Management*

D.R. Helliwell, *Options in Forestry*

D.R. Helliwell, *Planning for Nature Conservation*

J.A. Irving, *The Public in Your Woods*

J. Nix, P. Hill & N. Williams, *Land and Estate Management*

S. Owen, *Planning with Nature*

P.J. Stewart (ed), *The Wood for the Trees – the Debate about British Forestry*

THE
PATTERN
OF LANDSCAPE

Sylvia Crowe
and
Mary Mitchell

*"To read the landscape like a book, as well as to enjoy it as a picture,
opens the way to a new relationship between men and their environment.
The health of the landscape, its appearance and men's response to it
are interdependent."*

PACKARD PUBLISHING LIMITED
CHICHESTER

THE PATTERN OF LANDSCAPE

Copyright © Sylvia Crowe and Mary Mitchell 1988

First published in 1988 by Packard Publishing Limited,
16 Lynch Down, Funtington, Chichester, West Sussex
PO18 9LR, UK.

British Library Cataloguing in Publication Data

Crowe, Sylvia
     The pattern of landscape. — (Applied ecology, landscape
     and natural resource management series).
     1.   Landscape.   2.   Aesthetic aspects
     i. Title   ii. Mitchell, Mary, *1923*   iii. Series
     719'.01

ISBN 1 85341 019 5
ISBN 1 85341 020 9 pbk

Designed by Bruce Williams Designs, Chichester.

Production Team: June Cummings, Diana Dubens,
                    Michael Packard, Cecil Smith and
                    Bruce Williams.

Set in Palatino by CitySet Limited, Bosham, Chichester,
West Sussex PO18 8JU.

Printed and bound in Portugal by Printer Portuguesa Indústria
Gráfica Lda.

CONTENTS

*The photographs in this book illustrate the concepts described in the text and
are amplified by thematic captions. Reference is made to the illustrated concepts
and themes in the index. Specific locations are not consistently identified.*

PREFACE

I n compiling *The Pattern of Landscape* I am indebted to friends and colleagues in many countries who have been generous with their help and in giving permission to use their photographs. Mary Mitchell, who has compiled the illustrations, has been tireless in searching out and photographing examples of the various points I have wanted to make.

We are particularly indebted to Sue Jeeves who has generously allowed us access to the superb collection of photographs taken by her father, the late Stanley Jeeves.

If it appears that there is an undue preponderance of subjects for the British Isles, my excuse is, not only that I know the region better than any other, but also that within its small compass there is a remarkable variety of scenery, based on its complex geology, temperate climate and long settlement by man.

SC

PICTURE CREDITS

All photographs are by courtesy of Mary Mitchell except the following:
11, 27, 29, 30, 47, 60, 61, 64, 66, 79, 111, 125, 126, 131, 141, 147, 153 Sylvia Crowe;
5, 6, 7, 28, 52, 65, 81, 88, 101, 103, 138, 142, 143, 144 Stanley Jeeves;
33, 34, 72, 73, 130 Forestry Commission;
76, 157 Hugh Ingham;
13 Harry Causer;
19 Tom Turner;
21 Swiss Tourist Board;
37 Philip Lane;
38 George Anagnostopoulos;
39 KLM;
48 Andrew Besley;
62 TrekAmerica;
67 Cambridge University Collection of Air Photographs;
78 Richard Clough;
83 Ross Jackson;
121 Eric Meadows;
122 Marjory Whitehouse;
123 Pamela Jarman;
134 Arnold Lund (Oslo) – Norwegian National Tourist Office;
135 Irish Tourist Board;
137 Seb Nicholson.

INTRODUCTION

In different countries and at different times in history, men have looked at the landscape in various ways. It has been their home, their enemy, their God, their working partner or a storehouse to be plundered. All these attitudes to the environment can be found in the world today.

But there is also a dangerously superficial attitude which looks at the landscape as if it were a picture, unchanging and independent of the forces which influence it, a backcloth rather than a part of life. This attitude is recent and perhaps derives from the great numbers of articulate people who now look at landscapes without working or living in them.

It may also be influenced by the plethora of photographic representations in books and on the screen. These are enrichments of experience. But it must be recognized that there is a history and a living force behind the visual characteristics portrayed. Without this understanding, pictures of the landscapes of the whole planet may be brought before men's eyes without generating the will or the ability to conserve the fragile surface of the earth, still less to regenerate it. To attain these ends, there is a need today for a new appraisal of our attitude to our surroundings.

The scientific discoveries of the last century have revealed complexities in the world around us which were unknown to earlier ages. Faced with a vast universe, in which nothing is finite, simple or self-contained, men have a dual urge to probe all its mysteries and to find re-assurance in underlying laws which make its complexities comprehensible.

Responding to this quest, music and the visual arts explore ever more deeply into the unfamiliar and seek new meaning in apparent chaos and discord.

This search for order and meaning can find the landscape a living laboratory for studying the phenomenon of complexity within unity, for landscapes are infinitely varied, yet their structure and evolution follow immutable laws. Moreover, they show, not only the forces of nature at work, but also the effects of men's intervention, whether it be their inventiveness, their skill or their stupidity.

The growing power and numbers of the human race now influence the entire surface of the earth, if not by the destructive presence of men, then through their interference with climate, water, atmosphere and natural plant and animal communities.

In *The Pattern of Landscape* I have tried to trace the links between the physical functioning of the earth's surface and the response it evokes from men. Mankind's present preoccupation with mechanical and scientific skills, even reaching into the exploration of space, carries with it the need to strengthen our understanding and sense of kinship with our own home planet. If life on earth is to survive, men must understand the anatomy of landscape as well as they understand the workings of their own bodies, for they must now assume the responsibility of acting as the brain of evolution and the custodians of the earth.

1
Long ages of climatic action on the geologically ancient landscape of Cumbria, have carved the landscape into a dramatic composition of lakes and hills.

CHAPTER 1

THE
NATURE
OF LANDSCAPE

Every landscape has a pattern, formed by all its constituents and their relation to each other. As seen by the human eye, it is influenced by the quality of light and atmosphere, whether brilliant, subdued or misty. The constituents of the landscape are land and rock formation, vegetation and any structures men may put upon it.

It is the home of all terrestrial life.

Landscapes are not static. Changes may result from some sudden natural event, such as a volcanic eruption or an earthquake, or from drastic human intervention, in the flooding of a valley or the building of a city. Apart from these sudden changes the land is shaped gradually through thousands of years of climatic action and colonization by plants and animals.

These interacting factors produce a composite picture which can be interpreted into a geological, climatic and even social history of the land.

The surface of the earth reveals landscapes in every stage or evolution, from islands recently erupted from the sea, on which neither soil nor plants have yet developed, to worn-out landscapes such as the Libyan desert, whose past fertility has perished through natural and man-made erosion.

Between these extremes, lie the whole range of the earth's landscapes in varying stages of growth, maturity and decline, each revealing its own characteristic pattern.

Few areas remain untouched by man.

The basic form of landscapes result from geological and climatic action. They range from the drama of sea-cliffs and mountains to the placidity of plains, marshes and still water.

2
Different landscapes express different moods. Placidity is the keynote of these estuarial flats.

A single type of landscape may extend in linear form, as in mountain ranges, sea coasts or river valleys, or it may be centralized in a lake or mountain massif.

3
The long, narrow course of a river, develops a linear landscape.

4
When the river widens into a lake, the composition becomes centralized and static.

5,6
Just as in an artist's composition, a landscape may be dominated by a focal point or the pattern may be formed by juxtaposed elements.

Some types spread amorphously over great areas of the earth's surface, showing only local variations within an overall pattern. Deserts, tundra and tropical forests fall into this category.

A landscape may be seen as based on one focal point, or, it may be a composition of complementary forms.

The sculptural qualities of rock and landform depend on their geological origin and age and the climatic conditions governing their evolution. The results range from the sharply carved peaks of the Himalayas to the smooth moulding of the hills of south Scotland.

7
In geological terms, the
Himalayas are a young
formation. Time and weather
have not yet reduced their clean-
cut majesty.

8
In contrast the ancient hills of South Scotland have weathered down to a gentle, moulded form.

9
The limestone pavements of Western Ireland form a sculpture of bas-relief.

10
The English South Downs,
formed of soluble chalk, merge
with a gentle sweep into the flat
land of the Sussex Weald.

Many of the most distinctive landscape patterns develop along the line of transition between one formation and another.

The meeting of vertical and horizontal occurs at every scale, from the rise of tree trunks from the forest floor to the junction of hill and plain. The line of transition takes many forms, each with its own beauty. The Grand Tetons, rising sheer from the plain give a sense of drama, while there is peace and harmony in the gentle sweep of the South Downs into the Weald.

11
In contrast, the Grand Tetons,
in Wyoming, are formed of hard
rock and rise vertically from the
plain.

The transition from land to water forms the longest linear landscape on the earth's surface, ranging in character from the drama of cliffs to the flat sea-boards of marsh and estuary.

12,13
The longest linear landscape in the world is formed by sea coasts. They range in infinite variety from steep rugged cliffs to the gentle transition of marshland.

In the course of time, if the geological and climatic conditions are favourable, a patina will develop over the bare bones of rock formation.

Weathering, vegetation and the impact of animals produce a rich mosaic of shapes, colours and textures giving to different landscapes a grain of varying scales.

Different scales may be superimposed in one landscape. The apparently uniform surface of an upland plateau, monotonous at first glance, may reveal on close examination, the intricate pattern of minute alpines. A great forest imparts a large-scale pattern to the landform it covers, yet within it is a wealth of intimate detail.

14,15
Forests combine two scales. They may spread as an unbroken canopy of trees for hundreds of miles, yet they are made up of the intricate pattern of leaf and twig and the flowers and fungi of the forest floor.

The surface of a marsh appears homogeneous in the broad scale of an estuary but is made up of a rich mix of plant species arranged in a contrasting pattern of reed beds and reflecting water.

16,17
To the casual eye marshland stretches out in uniformity, but it is made up of the infinite variety of leaf, stem and pool.

18,19
The network is a recurring
pattern in nature. It may be
found on rocks or on a larger
scale, in the rivulets threading a
marsh.

Complementary to the mosaic structure, landscapes develop connecting networks, weaving the elements together into a tapestry. This pattern evolves on the weathering flanks of a mountain side, where vegetation creeps along the lines of fissure and stratification. The pattern is repeated where rivulets with their attendant growth articulate the plain.

A pattern of great beauty may develop where men work the land in sympathy with nature, adding the enrichment of new colours and textures to the mosaic without disrupting the harmony of nature's composition.

In the English Lake District the combined effects of a complex and ancient geological formation, a temperate climate, and long settlement by men, working and living in harmony with their surroundings, has produced a pattern of great diversity on an intimate scale which allows the contrast between rocky heights and green valleys to be brought within the

compass of the human eye. The reasons for this unique landscape stretch back over some four hundred million years. The great diversity of rock formations produced in this vast span of time and thrown up by past volcanic action, has resulted in the rich composition of contrasting forms. The long ages of weathering have reduced the mountains to an intimate scale. Climatic changes have cut features, such as Striding Edge, by the action of frost, smoothed out valleys by glacial action making them apt for cultivation, and given a long period of temperate climate, allowing the development of plant growth and a modest colonization by men.

20
In geological terms, the English Lake district is very old and weather has worn down the hills to a humanized scale, although the hard rocks retain their virility.

21,22
The Swiss Alps retain the scale and drama of their more recent formation, while the Cotswold hills reveal more soluble rock formation in the gentle contours of their hills and dales. A scene which is peaceful rather than dramatic.

In contrast, the equally diverse scenery of the Swiss Alps owes its far greater scale to a shorter time span since its volcanic formation.

The more uniform and recent geological formation of the Cotswolds shows a simpler and more uniform pattern. A scene of pastoral peace, rather than drama.

The influence of men on the landscape, spans the ages between the hunter, one more predator in the wild, to the city dweller within his self-created environment. Between these two extremes lie many degrees of relationship, each developing its own pattern of landscape.

Minimal impact can be seen in parts of West Africa where crops are grown beneath the canopy of the high forest, tended by villagers whose dwellings also shelter beneath the trees. The overall landscape of forest-clad land remains, only the internal pattern is humanized.

Beyond this minimal impact lie gradations of human influence as the partnership of man and nature develops. While the balance of the partnership is maintained, there is harmony between the humanized and the natural, each giving meaning and support to the other. From this relationship distinctive patterns develop.

In many Mediterranean countries the cultivated terraces merge into the maquis growth of the hillside, giving to the scene a sculptural quality. In mountainous lands cultivated fields in the valley floors accentuate the ruggedness of the flanking hills.

Men in these landscapes are working within the framework of natural ecosystems, increasing rather than depleting the biological diversity of the earth; and in doing so the visual richness is equally increased.

The attraction of edge, seen in the transition from hill to plain and land to water, is provided on a smaller scale by the transition from cultivated

23
In many parts of the world, men still find homes and livelihood within the forest which, treated with respect, will supply them indefinitely with food and shelter.

24
Vast areas of the earth's surface are patterned by men's agriculture. The age-old skill of terracing hillsides serves to conserve the soil, and forms a dramatic pattern of carved landscape.

25
On the island of St. Lucia infertile hills form a contrasting background to plantations of bananas in the rich valley soil.

land to natural surroundings, and between one crop and another, or a field and its boundary.

The juxtaposition of forest and cleared land not only gives contrast of colour and texture, solid and void, but also the strong feature of the forest edge with its many variations of form, from the soft billows of marginal undergrowth to the strong verticals of tree trunks.

26
Underlying geology is often revealed by vegetation. In this Cotswold scene, lines of trees grow along the ridges where the underlying rock strata comes too near the surface to allow for cultivation.

27
But there is beauty of a different kind, in the strong pattern of tree trunks rising cleanly from the ground.

Variations in a landscape on a scale comprehensible to the human eye usually result either from human activity, as in the formation of fields, or in local changes in the soil or underlying geological formation.

The exceptionally varied landscape of Britain is due both to its complex geological formation and to long human settlement. The reading of underlying geology through the pattern formed by vegetation and land use, can be seen in the Cotswolds, where drifts of woodland show where the underlying rock strata come too near the surface for easy cultivation. This gives a rhythmic pattern to a countryside of large-scale corn growing.

There comes a point where the enrichment of the landscape by diversification lapses into deterioration through fragmentation. The homogeneous character is lost and the natural habitats are reduced to a point where they neither are, nor appear, viable. This fragmentation is usually due to human intervention.

28
Edge, between one land use and another, is a significant landscape feature.
Undergrowth at the forest edge gives a gentle transition from vertical to horizontal.
Functionally, it checks the wind and encourages wild life.

29
Over many areas of the earth, the greed and ignorance of men have destroyed the landscape and the soil's fertility by overcropping.

30
But this scene in Japan shows that it is possible for intensive use by men to produce a landscape of quality and lasting fertility.

Provided the spirit and balance of partnership between man and nature is understood and maintained, human influence may be all-pervasive, changing from a pattern of human control within a background of untouched nature, to a man-controlled environment in which other species are tolerated, or actively cared for, by men. Increasing areas of the earth's surfaces are coming within this category. National Parks, through their care and control of wild life are, to a certain extent, man-manipulated.

In parts of Japan, intense human activity exists within a landscape of great natural beauty and ecological richness. On the fertile plain, shortage of land is used to the best advantage in producing food. The resulting pattern is a close patchwork of crops, fishponds and compact villages.

The agricultural landscape of Britain is a prototype of a partnership between man and nature which is found in varying forms in many parts of the earth's temperate zones. Man's control is evident throughout but there is great variation in the degree to which it reflects the character of the land and climate and makes provision for native species of plants and animals. In some cases the pattern has remained almost unchanged for centuries, but in others it has evolved as a result of new methods of cultivation and of men's changed outlook on life.

The hedges and copses of the old field pattern of lowland Britain were placed there by countrymen working with nature and following the dictates of climate and topography.

In contrast the legal enclosures of the late nineteenth century show

31
Past generations of Englishmen, knowing the qualities of their land and careful for the continuity of its fertility, laid out their fields in sympathy with contours, soil and climate.

straight, unresponsive lines set out by administrators divorced from the land, giving a pattern imposed on it rather than growing from it.

In general, the relationship of cultivation to natural factors has been weakened by the ability to overcome adverse growing conditions by the use of machinery, fertilizers and extensive drainage.

The copses and small woodlands which enriched many of the eighteenth and nineteenth century agricultural estates reflected the land-owner's desire to make the land his home; good to look at and to live in, and providing for his sport. Designed as habitats for fox and pheasant these woodlands served equally the needs of other wild life and, in so doing, gave a habitable look to the countryside as well as providing a varied ecology.

The old grazing system of small hedged fields gives a strongly humanized pattern of great appeal, but there can be a different kind of beauty in large, sweeping fields, bounded by belts of trees which give a greater sense of freedom and, often, of form. Both these patterns are suited to their purpose and each has a beauty of is own if it is good of its kind.

One of the reasons for the bleak appearance of some old agricultural landscapes from which hedges have been removed is that they have lost all sense of structure. They are obviously the torn remnants of a former pattern retaining only isolated trees and truncated hedges. An equal element of tree-cover disposed in a coherent pattern may create a land-scape of larger scale than the original but one which is still comprehensible and satisfying.

32
There is nostalgia for the pattern of small, hedged fields long considered typical of the English countryside. They were formed in response to changed methods of cultivation, and now further changes are sweeping them away into a new pattern of larger fields. But it is possible to develop a pleasant landscape if the fields are balanced by a generous planting of woodland and shelter belt.

33
Timber, like any other crop, must be harvested. If it is done with no thought for the landscape, it can create a ragged gash.

34
But with care and an eye for the country it gives the opportunity to open up views and woodland glades where the light let into the forest will generate a flush of woodland flowers.

In the same way a woodland clearing where a few isolated trees are left may appear ragged, while the same number of trees retained in groups related to the land form will give a look of coherence.

The typical pattern of agricultural landscapes is one of open space to which the third dimension is added in the shape of trees or hedges. This pattern takes many forms.

35,36
Agriculture in all its forms brings new patterns to the landscape. Scattered trees on the Cyprus hills form a patina of dots contrasting with the strong geometry of Portuguese olive orchards.

37
Long ago the fields of Kent were cut out from the wealden forest. Strips of this forest remain today as windbreaks between the orchards and hop gardens. Within them the forest flowers still flourish.

38
Geometry, imposed by agricultural man, can create a patterned landscape giving character to the land.

An overall pattern of dots is developed in orchards and olive groves. The wild prototype can be seen in the Savannah. Typical features of the eighteenth century English parklands are the clumps and single specimens of trees whose function was to give shade to browsing cattle. One group or single tree may form the focal point which gives distinction to a wide view.

In all these landscapes the trees are seen as features against a background of open space formed by land which has either been denuded of trees by former generations, or which was tree-less in its natural state.

A reverse pattern of open space carved out of tree-cover occurs where clearings are cut out of standing forest. The effect of this can be seen in the Weald of Kent and Sussex where the remaining strips of forest between the fields form a network of great beauty, rich in native flora and wild life.

On undulating terrain the attraction of patterns formed by agriculture depends largely upon the degree to which they inflect to its contours. On level ground they are more likely to be geometric. On the plain of Thessaly the great fields of corn are punctuated by the square blocks of almond orchard forming a strong geometric design.

39
In the polders, the Dutch have created new land reclaimed from the sea. They have added to it the woodlands and shelter belts needed in a windswept land.

All these patterns have evolved through men's work on existing landscapes. A further step in human control can be seen in the Dutch polders, man-made by reclamation from the sea. Here there are no natural features to deflect the geometric precision conceived by man's mathematical brain. Only two natural factors influence the pattern. The force of the wind makes sheltering trees for the homesteads a necessity and the recently acknowledged need to provide for fellow species has caused the introduction of some wildlife habitats in the form of small woodlands.

40
In Israel's Heulah Valley a new landscape has been created by the method of reclaiming land from the desert by irrigation.

A pattern as geometric as the polders has evolved in Israel's Heulah valley. Here some connection with natural landscape is given by its setting within the surrounding scrub-covered hills, and a length of old water-way has been conserved in its natural state as a nature reserve.

These diverse landscapes are all capable of sustained life. They all share a pattern of water, soil and vegetation, forming a habitat for men and other species. This viable mosaic can be developed with an increasing degree of humanization even into the urban landscape. But just as an urban pattern can degenerate into an amorphous mass lacking both cohesion and differentiation, so the rural landscape can lose its mosaic structure and revert to the lifeless surface of newly created land – full circle from desolation to desolation.

This reversion is sometimes effected by natural causes, volcanic action or aridity of climate. But it is most frequently caused by a breakdown in the partnership between man and nature. These dead landscapes have lost all organic structure. Any appeal they may have is a purely visual impact of form and drama.

All landscapes derive from the basic facts of nature, sometimes modified by man seeking home and livelihood. But there are also landscapes visibly dominated by man's aspirations. Modern versions of the landscape dominated by thought, are seen in the structures for space communication. These appear to float unrelated above the landscapes in which they stand, unlike the earlier manifestation of thought, which though aspiring to heaven, were rooted firmly in the earth like the rock-based temple of Jerusalem and the cathedrals of medieval Europe.

41
Vast areas of the earth's surface are covered by almost lifeless wastelands. Some have become so in the course of nature, but many are the result of men's actions such as these china-clay waste tips.

42
Even areas of desolation may have a dramatic appeal, as in this worked-out slate quarry in the Welsh hills.

43,44
The new dimension which space exploration has brought to human thinking is reflected in the radar spheres on the Yorkshire moors. Unrelated to the organic earth, they reflect man's new air-borne exploration – an age away from the earth-bound strength of Bamburgh Castle, rooted in the rock on which it stands.

45,46
*Since water is the life-blood of
the Israeli Kibbutz, it is fitting
that the water tower dominates
the sky line, while its tight-knit
community is expressed in a
domesticity akin to suburbia.*

The Israeli Kibbutz, rooted very firmly in the earth, is also the expression of an idea, that of the achievement of man in a harsh environment. It expresses too, the regeneration of a degraded landscape back to its legendary state of paradise.

The expression of the thought is the water tower, source of life, rising as a focal point within the vast scale of desert and reclaimed fields, and, within the small-scale domesticity of the common garden, expressing the tight-knit unity of the community.

47
Works of civil engineering
which relate to natural forces,
sit happily within the landscape
provided their design is simple,
functional and related to their
surroundings. Attempts at
decoration or any triviality
destroy the relationship.

48
The wild character of a rugged
coast is emphasized by the
lonely lighthouse, but would be
desecrated by a bungalow.

All landscapes dominated by thought or aspiration have a strong emotional appeal. This appeal may extend in a more mundane form to landscapes where the essential character of the terrain has been harnessed to men's service.

Hydro-electric and irrigation schemes can express the geological character and scale of their sites with simplicity and grandeur. Their beauty depends on the clarity with which the relationship between land-form and function is expressed. Both the natural landscape and the idea of power production are on the grand scale. Their unity is disrupted by details related to the human scale, unless these are an integral part of the whole, as a leaf is an integral part of the forest.

The clean simplicity of a light-house, organic in form as if growing from the rock, highlights the rugged dangers of the coast.

49
The impersonal structure of a nuclear power station rises from a landscape neither wild nor humanized. In scale and architecture it stands aloof from the organic world.

Industrial landscapes which have neither the airborne appearance of the space installation nor any functional relation to their site often bring incongruity to the countryside, particularly if they are based on the needs of a large human population unrelated to the land. They can, however, create an entirely new type of landscape neither urban nor wild.

The strongest purely visual element in a landscape is the composition of form, whether it be the strong pattern of mountain peaks against the sky or the floating shapes of water and woodland on the plain or the small-scale compositions of rock and vegetation.

50,51,52
Patterns in the landscape range in scale, strength and character from rugged mountain peaks against the sky, through the gentle floating shapes of sand and water (left), down to the intricate patterns of rock and vegetation.

53
Small-scale compositions of rock and vegetation are complemented by a bridge in scale and keeping with the setting.

54
The textures within a landscape are as varied and as important as its colours. The coarse texture of a rock fall emphasizes the rough character of a hillside. While a sheep-bitten turf conveys a sense of peace.

55
The pleasure given by the pattern of ordered cultivation is accentuated by the contrast of tangled scrub. Without some contrast of natural growth, endless cultivated fields may be monotonous.

56,57
The plants and animals of the countryside are interdependent. In English woodlands rabbits keep down the coarse growth of bramble and thicket and allow the woodland flowers to flourish. The grazing of sheep on the South Downs produces the short even turf which allows the growth of thyme, scabious and orchid.

But in all cases colour and texture not only play their part in defining the shapes of a composition, but in their own right may form the essence of a landscape.

Landscape textures range from the coarse grained geological formations of rock falls to the smoothness of sheep-bitten turf. The tangle of scrub contrasts with the cultivated field, the cacti with the fine sand of the desert.

Texture is influenced by animals, both wild and domesticated. Wild deer graze the forest glades whose fine turf contrasts with the rough texture of the oak. Rabbits may ensure an open, flower-studded forest floor, which with their extinction, becomes a bramble thicket. Where horse and cattle have replaced sheep on the South Downs the smooth turf has turned to coarse grass, obliterating the small downland flowers.

58
The elimination of rabbits by myxomatosis and the replacement of sheep by cattle, with their coarser grazing habits, caused deterioration of the flora.

59,60
Colour is dependent on the quality of light as well as upon pigment, the misty climate gives Ireland its soft colours, while the brilliance of the Isles of Greece reflect their sunny clime.

The form and texture of a landscape are relatively constant. Light and colour are ever changing. Yet certain ranges of colour and qualities of light appertain to individual landscapes.

The west coast of Ireland, distinctive in form with its small scale, beautifully shaped hills and indented coast-line, yet owes much of its unique character to the quality of light radiating from the Atlantic seaboard over which roll the great banks of cloud. This gives to the hills and the bogs from which they rise a soft colouring which is yet deep and intense. It is far removed from the brilliant light of the Isles of Greece and even from the mistier atmosphere of the English Lakes; landscapes to which it might otherwise bear some resemblance.

There are landscapes whose form is only revealed at sunrise and sunset. The apparent uniformity of the Sahara desert is transformed into a pattern of rose and heliotrope when the rising sun throws shadows from its undulations. A similar transformation is seen looking down into the

61,62
Strong light can deaden colour. At midday the Grand Canyon is almost dull. At dawn and dusk it is revealed as a great coloured sculpture (above).

Grand Canyon; featureless at midday, it is transformed into a great sculpture at dawn and dusk.

In distant landscapes colouring depends almost entirely on light and atmosphere, but in the foreground and middle distance the colours of rock, soil and vegetation strike the dominant note. Often their juxtaposition gives vivid contrasts.

63,64
The Western Australian desert reveals simple and striking compositions and colour schemes. The red sand forms a perfect setting for the grey-green vegetation.

In the Western Australian desert the brilliant red soil contrasts with the silver-grey plants. In quieter contrast the deep green of a fern lies against the grey Cumbrian rock, and the silvery sand dunes form the background to the grey-green of Marram grass.

The tapestry of different colours disappears under monoculture and weed-free agriculture. The intense but unchanging green of improved pasture is a dull substitute for the flower-rich meadows of an earlier age in

England or the alpine pastures of Switzerland. An equal deprivation is the replacement of deciduous woodlands by pure coniferous forests.

Science confirms the objections to monoculture which are sensed by the eye, for it increases susceptibility to disease and impoverishes the soil. Stapleton, in *The Land To-day and To-morrow*, published in 1935, already foresaw the danger, and advocated amongst other conservation measures, the retention of strips of wild herbage within the pattern of cultivation.

65
In the cool, moist climate of northern England, deep green ferns lie against grey rocks.

While Nature too, has apparent monocultures, within her main crop there are always subsidiary species. In the coniferous forests of Colorado, natural fires open up spaces in the canopy which are colonized by aspen whose golden autumn foliage lights up the dark expanse of forest.

The earth's landscape reflects the immense diversity of evolution. It is an amalgam of elements of varying scales and character, from the minute

66
The aspen is a weed in Colorado forests, colonizing areas cleared by forest fires. But the flaming orange of its autumn colour is a welcome break in the expanse of dark conifer.

pattern of the moss to the mountain massif.

Of all the earth's species, only man has the capacity to recognize and understand the value of each separate component in producing the total environment. This capacity lays upon him an immense responsibility which so far he has failed to accept.

CHAPTER 2

THE
LANDSCAPE
AS A HABITAT

A good' landscape might be defined as an interwoven complex of habitats, together forming a scene of beauty. The landscape in its widest sense, comprises the whole surface of the earth. It is the home of all terrestrial species and within it must be found a place for every type of life. To achieve this a landscape of great complexity is needed, rich in contrasts of scale and character, eschewing uniformity. In common with other organisms, the landscape is made up of cells, forming together an ever larger and more complex entity.

To function efficiently, each component cell must be healthy and in the right relationship to the whole. Superimposed on this cell structure and dependent upon it, the pattern of habitats is one of overlapping, intersecting zones. The scale of these zones varies from the single bush, adequate for a nesting blackbird, to the huge range of jungle needed by a herd of elephants. Certain birds of the Amazonian rain forest need a territory of 2500 square kilometres.

Each zone is not an isolated island, but part of an interwoven tapestry providing in its complex pattern the living conditions for all the species which form the food-chain up to the higher animals.

Gradually, knowledge is being acquired of the living space and conditions needed by all species. The breeding, hunting and feeding territories of animals, their tolerance of interference and the minimum viable size of a breeding colony of plants or animals, is basic to the pattern of a landscape. There is a maximum distance beyond which a bird will not fetch food for its young, a bee forage for nectar or a carnivore hunt for its prey. These space requirements are as relevant to land planning as human living conditions are to town planning.

Some habitats may appear as large areas of uniformity, and yet contain a wide variety of interdependent habitats. Such are the tropical forests and sea marshes, both habitats of great richness. The wide, simple unity of a moorland contains a great variety of life forming a food-chain, culminating perhaps in the shrew, which in turn, is the food of the kite, circling overhead.

Contrasting with these overall patterns are the strongly articulated landscapes showing a network pattern, whose nodes form the main habitats, linked by a system of passages. This is exemplified in the traditional English agricultural landscape. Copses, woodlands, heaths and ponds form the nodes or islands, hedges, shelter belts and ditches; the connecting network. The mirror pattern of fields intersected by hedges is a forest intersected by rides. These too, are the passage ways for many species of bird, plant and animal.

A modification of the node and passage pattern is that of islands, without the connecting network. This serves adequately for birds and wind-

67
Wild life habitats within the landscape may form a pattern of islands, serving as homelands for varying species.

blown seeds, but not for earthbound species, unless the intervening distance is short and navigable. The size and character of the nodes or islands and their relationship to each other, governs the wild life they support.

Research at Monks Wood, in England, has identified the varying sizes of woodland needed by different species of bird. A blackcap for example, only requires a minimum of 300 square metres, while a woodpecker needs two hectares. These woods are likened to islands, set in a sea of agriculture. A similar term is applied to ponds, where again size may determine the species occupying them. A moorhen is content to nest on a pond of 10 square metres, and find its food on land, while a great crested grebe requires over one hectare to both nest and feed.

This research has also underlined the importance of retaining relatively large areas of undisturbed habitat and the dangers of over-fragmentation. A tenfold increase in a wood's area has been found to double the number of species. The pattern of such variously sized islands, in different groupings, produces landscapes of great interest and beauty.

The human equivalent of a landscape rich in habitats, is the city, where each type of life and activity has its own requirement of space and character of the environment.

The road system is the equivalent of the landscape's connecting links; in neither case must they be severed.

But while the city is built for men, it also serves as the home for many other species. Many different birds live and nest in the London area, for example. Enlightened town planning will not only provide open spaces attuned to conservation, which will form the nodes of a system of habitats, but will also guard the health of waterways and the continuity of greenways which form the arteries serving wild life as well as pedestrians. A well-planned city shows nature's pattern of cell and artery. The principle of co-existence between men and other species, upon which depends the future of life on this planet, must extend through towns as well as countryside.

While the pattern of islands and that of the node and network are static, a third pattern, that of the branching tree is one of growth and movement. It is a recurring form in nature and an oak tree may be taken as a prototype. *Quercus robor* may support over 2000 species of insect, bird and mammal on its connected network of root, trunk, branch and leaf; each organism providing food for other forms of life. Each leaf repeats the trees branching pattern on a miniature scale.

The valleys of a mountain range are a larger version of the same pattern. These provide habitats for hill and valley species, interacting and mutually supporting, while the area as a whole, may be the living zone for wide-ranging animals and birds.

The pattern appears again in a river system with its tributary streams and its final delta. In its course, the river provides a series of habitats, each reflected in the ever-changing scene. The fast-running, rocky course of its upper reaches, is the habitat for dippers and spawning salmon. In its lower meanders it deposits fertile silt from which on one side springs rich herbage, while on the other side, it cuts into the bank to create sites for otters' holts and the nests of kingfishers. The riffles over the stones washed down from the upper reaches are a favourite haunt of trout.

At its estuary the river widens into mud flats, the feeding grounds for wading birds and providing in their marshy terrain one of the richest of all biosystems.

The diversity of riverine life and the need it satisfies for different species would appear to be infinite, yet the river is one connected, interacting whole, constantly in movement, yet with all its parts interdependent. It illustrates the truth that no landscape is a single, static unit cut out from its surroundings with a definite boundary line but rather a continuous organic phenomenon, a Chinese scroll rather than a framed picture.

The river's adaptation for life has evolved through millions of years and is taken for granted. Yet any new factor may destroy the delicate balance which lies at the root of its harmony and life. A canalized stretch of river will destroy the haunts of otter and kingfisher, the removal of bankside trees robs the trout of his flies and a myriad of organisms of their food and shelter. Pollution which may be from distant sources can end all life.

Landscapes which lack a rich articulation of habitats have a meagre and inhospitable look unless the sheer drama of their geological formation provides compensation for paucity of life. But even here the addition of life adds a new dimension to the grandeur of the scene.

This correlation between visual interest and habitat appears in woodlands. A conifer monoculture, by many found visually dull, is attractive as

68
Streams and rivers are the landscape's arteries of life. Near the stream's source may be found spawning salmon and a dipper's nest.

69
Otters and kingfishers will find haunts along the steep river banks.

70
Where the river slows its course and widens into an estuary it deposits silt carried down its course, forming marshlands and shallows which are colonized by wading birds.

71
Kittiwakes crowd the steep cliffs in the Farne Islands, which not only provide ideal nesting sites, but rise from water rich in fish.

72,73
Varying types of forest serve the needs of many species. Open glades are favoured by the browsing deer while deep thickets provide the nightingale with nesting sites.

a habitat to relatively few species of bird, notably, in Great Britain, the fire-crest and capercaillie, while the more visually attractive mixed woodlands are rich in species of plant, animal and bird.

Mixed age is as conducive as mixed species to variety of habitats. Open forest floor beneath high forest will be colonized by flowers while in other places the thicket stage of growth and woodland shrubs give nesting places for nightingales and warblers.

The whole forest plan can contribute to this dual benefit of visual pleasure and rich wild life. The occasional wide ride lets in the sun to encourage wild flowers, which in their turn, will bring the butterflies. Space for natural growth around ponds and beside streams encourages aquatic life and gives the pleasure of seeing the dragonflies. Deer come to graze on open grassy glades and shrubs at the forest edge are favoured as nesting sites by many small birds. The occasional dead tree should be spared. It is often a picturesque incident, but more importantly, it is needed by the woodpecker.

The tendency to groom a landscape into tidiness can lead to impoverishment. The cut face of an abandoned sand-pit is the sand martin's home. A disused chalk quarry is rich in lime-loving flowers and their attendant

74
Too much tidiness can sterilize a landscape. The woodpecker needs the occasional dead tree for its nesting hole.

insects. The odd patch of nettles is essential to the caterpillars of the red admiral and peacock butterflies, goldfinches rejoice in the seeds of thistle-heads. Ivy does not kill its host tree, it shelters it and gives nesting places for birds and a late feed for bees. This constant human desire to clean and control nature, is at its most acute in agricultural practices. The balance

between efficient food production and the maintenance of a healthy landscape is a delicate one and needs constant vigilance, foresight and research.

The increase in human population with its ever-increasing demand for

75
*Ivy clothing a ruined wall
provides a late feed for bees.*

food, makes it urgent to plan for this balance in all parts of the earth. There
must be co-existence between men and other species, if life on earth is to
continue.

Short-term agricultural benefits may often be outweighed by long-term
damage to the land. The most dramatic instances are seen in the deserts
and dust bowls, but even fertile land in temperate climates may suffer. For
example, in many river valleys water meadows occupy the flood plain,
allowing riverside trees to remain as shade for the cattle. This peaceful
scene, responding to the facts of nature, is destroyed when ploughed land
for cereals is brought close to the river banks, defying risk of flood and
destroying tree cover to the detriment of the river and its fish.

There is constant interaction between habitats and their living popu-
lations. In the wild it ranges from the dramatic action of beavers and
trampling herds of elephant, to the ceaseless control and propagation of
plants by birds, animals and insects.

But the greatest changes are wrought by men and by the animals they
introduce to different parts of the world. Over-grazing by goats, sheep and
cattle have completely changed the landscape in many parts of the world.
Once the Isles of Greece and the Highlands of Scotland were forest-clad, as
were many of today's deserts.

The rich fauna and flora of an ancient woodland have developed over
centuries, or even millenia. They cannot be re-created within a short life-
time. Research on the old hedgerows of the English countryside, has
found that a 200-year old hedge averages two species of shrub per 30
yards, while one 1000 year-old will have 10 species in the same length.

Newly planted woods and hedges, welcome as they are, form no true
replacement for those lost. Ancient pastures show a similar richness of
species, irreplaceable once destroyed. Change there must be, but its true
cost should be realized. An ancient plant community deserves quite as
much protection as an ancient building. The maintenance of the surface of
the earth as a habitat should be the first priority in men's endeavours, for
without it mankind will have no future and little pleasure in the present.

CHAPTER 3

THE
HUMAN
RESPONSE

A definition of beauty has long been sought and no final answer has been given, nor is one likely to be found.

It is particularly difficult to apply rigid criteria to landscape for the response of the beholder is infinitely variable and not solely visual. It is deeply emotional and concerns all the senses; scent, sound and touch all play their part.

To an artist, a scene may be purely a composition of shapes, colours and textures. But others may see it with the eyes of a farmer, a geologist or a historian. Emotions, memories and historic associations all play their part and modify the purely visual reaction. The difficulty of defining an objective view is illustrated by the well-known changes in taste over the ages for different types of landscape, ranging from revulsion against the wild in the eighteenth century to its adulation by the picturesque movement a century later. The latter's condemnation of a 'smooth' landscape would presumably have ruled out of favour the short turf of the South Downs. Due, perhaps to world-wide travel, the present age takes a more balanced and catholic view, finding beauty in a diversity of scenes. Personal

76,77
Familiar laws of composition are exemplified in the landscape. The vertical spire of a church rises from the horizontal line of fields. In a wilder context, cactus rises from the Arizona desert (left).

preferences will always remain, but there are certain moods and patterns which have an almost universal appeal.

The purely visual aspects of a landscape are the easiest to assess because they can be judged by long-established criteria of composition and colour. Certain compositions which please the eye recur in a diversity of scale and form.

The simple statement of a vertical rising from a horizontal plane is seen

78
In a Canberra park, poplars contrast with still water.

in a church rising from level fields, a cactus rising from the desert and a poplar contrasting with a sheet of water. A development of this theme is the grouping of vertical, recumbent and horizontal, a traditional feature of Japanese art. A tree is added to the church, a rock to the cactus, a willow to the poplar.

79,80
Compositions are enriched by
the addition of a tree to the
church, a willow beside a
poplar.

A view may be focused and enhanced by framing. This may be by the arch of a bridge, by trees meeting over a sunken lane, a vista down an avenue or even by the side of a steep valley.

In these tunnelled views, the shape of the terminal opening is the heart of the composition, led up to by the strength or subtlety of the approach.

81,82
Just as a picture is emphasized by framing, a view is intensified when seen through the arch of a bridge. The steep banks of a lane heighten the expectation.

83
The framing of the flanking hills and the lead-in of the valley stream concentrates the view on the focal point of the hills. Whatever forms the frame, the heart of the composition is its terminal view.

84
A variant of the frame is the grill. The trunks of trees accentuate the view.

85
The same attraction gives the childish pleasure of lying at the edge of a field and looking through the stems of plants.

A variant of the frame is the distancing of a view seen through a grill, which may be formed by tree trunks, branches or even by the stems of grasses.

Penetration, leading the eye into a view, may be achieved by a winding river, a track or a drift of trees.

86,87
The eye may be drawn into a view by a river, or a drift of trees.

The strength of a composition may depend on the character of its focal object, a tree, a building, a mountain or a single rock.

Sometimes the composition is of complementary forms, making together a unified group.

The repetitive man-made pattern of a viaduct or colonnade, occurs in looser form in the serried ranks of tree trunks. A less formal version is seen in the rhythmic dip and scarp of tilted strata on a mountain skyline, or in the wave formation of windblown sand dunes.

Hilltop villages or clumps of trees make a landscape memorable by accentuation.

88,89
The strength of a view lies in its focal point; it may be a tree, or a mountain peak, or an evocatively shaped rock.

90
*A composition within the
landscape may be a group of
complementary forms, like a
picture by Braque.*

91,92
*In contrast to the static
composition, the eye may travel
along a rhythmic line of
repetition, as in a viaduct or in
nature's counterpart, a serried
rank of tree-trunks.*

93
*In a less rigid but grander form,
the Seven Sisters of Kintail run
along the skyline.*

94
*Wind-blown sand dunes in
Qatar, give the same sense of
rhythmic progression.*

95,96
The eye is always drawn to focal points on hilltops, whether it is a fortified hill village or a clump of trees.

97,98,99
The links between the tenets of
art and the laws of nature may
be long debated but undoubtedly
Hogarth's 'Line of Beauty' can
be found in many natural forms;
the branch of a tree, the line of a
water channel or, interpreted by
an engineer, in the sweep of a
harbour wall.

100,101,102
The mosaic has been an artistic
motif through the ages.
Nature's versions can be in
shingle on the beach, in the
pattern made by rocks and
vegetation or leaves against
the sky.

103,104,105
Recurrent types of composition
can be recognized in many
different forms and varying
scales. The pattern of mountain
peaks is echoed in miniature by a
group of rocks, or even in the
pattern of a gnarled tree trunk.

Forms long recognized in art appear in many different guises in the landscape. The serpentine line of beauty may be a water course, a curving branch or a sculptured valley.

The mosaic structure developed by mature landscapes is a pattern easily grasped by the human eye.

It appears at many different scales from shingle on the beach and leaves against the sky, to rocks and vegetation on a hillside, sometimes enriched by the intake of a hill farm.

The landscapes most easily appreciated are those whose pattern is revealed on a large scale, as in the strong grouping of a mountain range, but the same composition can be discerned on a smaller scale in the grouping of rocks or the carving of a gnarled tree.

Once again this contrast of scale can be seen in the forest. Within the overall pattern of its canopy, lies a pattern of infinite variety of form, texture and colour. The network of branches make a composition of arches, frets, spirals and rhomboids. Textures range from deep mosses and the smooth spheres of toadstools to the fissured bark of trees; the spectrum of colours stretches over every shade of brown and green to the brilliance of spring flowers and autumn leaves.

106
On the forest floor fallen leaves
form a pattern of contrast with
the smooth toadstools.

107
Within the wide scale of the
forest canopy a host of intricate
patterns are formed by
interweaving twigs and
branches.

Elsewhere the interaction of opposing forces can produce patterns where the tension is resolved into a unity of composition. Sun rings on the water broken by wave action, rocks deflecting the course of falling water, produce patterns of intricacy and movement.

A more static pattern of opposing forces is seen in the landscape of sea-worn cliffs cutting into the smooth turf formed by ages of surface weathering and stabilization.

108
On the Sussex coast, the smooth sheep-bitten turf contrasts with the steep chalk cliffs, cut by ages of sea action.

109,110
*The forces of nature form
patterns in the landscape.
Mobile patterns range from the
gentle shimmering of sun-rings
on the sea to fast-running
mountain streams.*

111
A strong pattern, man-made
but in tune with natural forces,
is produced by ski slopes on the
Colorado mountains.

Because the factors of landscape are so complex, there is an immediate response to patterns which show clearly the forces which have produced them. The drama of the Grand Canyon is an overwhelming statement of natural forces expressed with sublime simplicity. In a more subtle mood so are the shapes formed by the action of waves and currents on the sand.

This clarity of expression is one of the many attractions of water. It emphasizes the laws of nature, whether as a still lake marking the lowest point of a valley floor, a torrent dramatizing the sheer cliff, or a flooded rice terrace showing the precise contouring of a gentler hill.

A woodland pool, reflecting the deep colours of the forest, and a mountain tarn holding a brilliant mirror to the sky, accentuate, respectively, the woodland depths and the mountain heights.

112,113
The repetitive pattern created by
nature is seen in the wave
formation of wavelets in an
estuary or wind-blown sand
dunes.

114,115
The forms which water takes in the landscape are infinite and each has its own appeal. The tranquillity of a still lake contrasts with the turmoil of a waterfall.

116
In Japan the flooded rice fields
pattern the valley floor.

117,118
There is mystery in the
shadowed depth of a woodland
pool and exhilaration in the
light-reflecting hill-top tarn.

119,120
The stillness of a millpond
contrasts with breakers on the
Cornish coast.

121
Plough furrows create a sweeping pattern in a flat agricultural landscape.

Wind, bird-song and water are the three elements which bring sound and movement to the landscape, and the most constant of these is water. Its moods are infinite, from the utter stillness of a mill pond to the exhilaration of sea breakers and waterfalls.

Response is quickened to a landscape which strikes a chord of recognition or a sense that it illustrates some underlying truth. No pattern illustrates this more clearly than contour ploughing or terracing. The pattern would be good if it were merely a piece of sculpture, but there is the added attraction of the clarity with which the contour lines accentuate the land form, and show how closely man has worked with nature.

122
*Man's activity has added the
sculptural pattern of terraced
fields to a landscape in the
Indian hills.*

Landscapes showing the partnership of man with nature are amongst
the most beautiful and evocative in the world. The mosaic of the earth's
surface is enriched by changes of colours and texture introduced by agriculture. New forms emerge showing the inflection of men's geometry to
nature's organic forms. To this visual enrichment is added the emotional
appeal of kinship with those who have worked the land.

In these humanized landscapes where men and nature have co-
operated, patterns of great beauty may emerge. These are exemplified by
the swing of plough furrows in an English field, the serried rows of olive
trees on a Spanish hill, the ranks of peat ('turf') stacks on an Irish bog and
the rhythmic lines of brushwood planted as sea and wind defence on
North Sea sand dunes.

Perhaps most evocative of all is the carving of an amphitheatre in the
Grecian hills.

There is an emotional response where man or nature herself has
prevailed against adverse conditions. A lone tree rising triumphant from
the desert adds this appeal to intrinsic dignity of form. An oasis, with its
green trees and minaret appearing suddenly from the inhospitable desert
has the same quality of visual beauty heightened by emotional appeal; in
this case, a recognition of human achievement and divine supremacy.

Wind force is a potent cause of the struggle for existence, both for men
and other species. Windclipped cushions of alpines on mountain tops and
sculptured cliff-top vegetation are patterns of hardiness as well as satisfying compositions of form. Windblown trees shape themselves almost
mathematically to the force of the wind, making an objectively satisfying
shape whose appeal is intensified by the intimation of successful adaptation to external force.

123
*Turf stacks on an Irish bog bring
a formal pattern to a wild
landscape.*

124
*Bales of straw break the expanse
of a field of stubble.*

125
*The rhythmic pattern of
brushwood planted to stabilize
the shifting sand dunes echoes
the natural forces of wind and
sea which it is combating.*

126
*There is unfailing appeal in the
sight of survival in the face of
odds. The lone tree rising from
the Australian desert means
more than a whole forest in a
fertile land.*

127
*The Turkish amphitheatre adds
the emotional appeal of history
to its intrinsically beautiful
form.*

128,129
*Wind-clipped vegetation
clinging to the cliff is a symbol of
the will to survive in a gale
whose force is revealed also in
the angle of the wind-swept
tree.*

130
The British Isles bear the force of the Atlantic gales; strips of woodland shelter fields in the Scottish Borders.

131
In the gentler but still windswept climate of the Isles of Scilly, hedges shelter the fields of early daffodils.

132
A tree clings for survival to a
rock face.

The patterns resulting from men's efforts to gain shelter, range from the free curves of wide-spaced shelter belts on Britain's northern hills to the close, precise pattern of hedges sheltering spring bulbs from the Atlantic gales in the Isles of Scilly.

Rectangular belts of woodland punctuate agricultural plains in Brazil making a bold, large-scale pattern, while in Egypt a thin line of casuarina trees protect and shade the irrigation channels. Each form interprets the climate and the land.

Intimations of struggle heighten response to the beauty of a gnarled tree-trunk clinging to a rock face, or a patriarchal oak tree defying age on a village green.

Men's successful efforts against odds is epitomized in the landscape of the Norwegian fiords, a magnificent composition of form and colour. The strength of the hills dropping steeply into the dark waters is both dramatic and visually superb, but an extra dimension is added where a small white farmhouse clings to the base of the rock with its bright green field taking up the minute area of level ground between mountain and water.

A less dramatic, but strongly patterned version of the same urge to wrest a living from hard conditions, appears in the West of Ireland, where stones have been gathered both to clear the minute fields and to build for them sheltering walls.

The obverse of the appeal of struggle is the sense of harmony where man or nature has responded to favourable conditions. Common throughout the temperate world is the pattern of wooded hillsides sheltering valleys. This is in part a natural pattern where trees grow above the flood-plain and below the windswept hill-tops and in part a man-made one where trees are planted to protect crops and dwellings from wind and avalanche.

The course of a valley is often accentuated by a line of trees along the riverside. This may result from natural growing conditions or because the cultivation of the valley fields cannot easily be brought up to the water's edge. This tree growth is important to the health of riverine life as well as an enrichment of visual landscape. There is a striking example in a largely treeless area of New South Wales, where willows have been planted along small streams in the valley bottoms; the work of one man of vision, a clergyman who rode his parish with willow cuttings in his pocket; a modern example of John Evelyn's service to the English countryside with his pocketful of acorns.

The emotional appeal of familiar sights shows itself in the widespread opposition to change. A positive side of this negative attitude is the pleasure of recognition when a pattern recurs in different forms. The veins of a leaf, the branches of a tree and the rivulets of a delta are all versions of a fundamental pattern examplified in our own circulatory system.

133
A walnut tree defies time on a village green.

Network patterns give a sense of intimacy and reassurance, measuring and containing the space they cover. This again is one of the attractions of the hedged fields of traditional English agriculture. A lattice of twigs against the sky gives the same pattern on a small scale. As the twigs and branches carry the sap of the growing tree, the hedgerows carry the wild life of the countryside, and irrigation channels carry life to the desert.

134,135
Man finds a precarious foothold
on the edge of a Norwegian fjord
and has the tenacity to clear
stones from the small fields of
Ireland to build walls against
the Atlantic gales.

136
Trees accentuate the landform of
the valley.

137
Certain patterns in nature are
recurring. Rivulets irrigating a
plain are similar in purpose and
in form to the veins of the
human hand.

138,139,140
The network is a recurring
pattern. It can be seen in the
lattice of twigs against the sky,
and in hedges reticulating the
traditional English farmland
and in drainage channels in
marshland.

The pattern of islands composed of individual shapes silhouetted against a level surface occurs in many forms.

The Isles of Scilly, rising from the sea, Suilven and Canisp rising from the Scottish moors, or on a smaller scale, lilypads floating on the surface of a lake, are all versions of this theme whose appeal lies in the composition

141
The pattern of islands recurs in many forms. Seen from the air, the Isles of Scilly are a prototype.

of their grouping, the distinction of their form and the unifying quality of the background. Perhaps the most evocative version of all, is the climber's reward of seeing mountain-tops floating like islands above a sea of clouds.

The moods evoked by landscapes are the most personal response of all. Yet even these are largely predictable. The sense of freedom and exhilaration inspired by the wide views from a mountain top is almost universal and the same feeling in a lower key is given by views over plains and the open sea.

The mood is intensified by a sail on the sea or a lone tree on the plain. It is destroyed by a scatter of incongruous objects. Power lines criss-crossing the desert outside Cairo turns the awesome experience of a desert waste into a scene of squalor. The sublimity of a mountain scene is destroyed by a multiplicity of ski-lifts but enhanced by a small farmhouse held protectively within the mountain structure.

The longing for the freedom of wide open spaces exists side by side with a desire for safe containment. The strength of these opposing ideas ranges from the dread of a cave felt by claustrophobics to an agoraphobic's dislike of open space. Between these two extremes, the average man seeks alternately, the safety of enclosure and the freedom of space; a large-scale version of the architectural principle of alternate contraction and expansion.

These diverse demands of the human temperament are met in the

142,143
A land-based version of the pattern of islands shows Suilven and Canisp rising from the Highland moors, and (left) most evocative of all, mountain peaks rising above a sea of cloud.

144
Lily pads floating on the water bring the pattern down to peace and domesticity.

145,146,147
Human impact on a landscape can enhance it or destroy it. A lone sailing boat intensifies the sea's appeal, mountains give protection to farm buildings, while a pumping unit can insult the rugged beauty of a hillside.

148
A seat at the woodland's edge combines a feeling of security with the freedom of an open view.

149,150
The permeable enclosure of a
woodland contrasts with the
solid more rigid enclosure of a
rocky gorge.

endless variety of the earth's landscape. The shelter of a great rock, the edge of a forest or a hollow in the foothills, combine the security of enclosure with the freedom of a wide view. The same reconciliation of freedom with security accounts for the predilection for the seat against the wall and the picnic spot at the woodland's edge.

Space division and the interpenetration of void and solid takes many forms. The permeable enclosure formed by trees within a woodland contrasts with the solid wall of a gorge.

The in-and-out progression may be formed loosely by groupings of trees, by rides in a forest or, with greater emphasis, by the opening up of gorges into wide valleys or narrow streams debouching into lakes.

While the extrovert seeks the expansive mood of deserts, sea and mountain, and the romantic looks for rocky crags and the mysteries of deep valleys, those with a more domestic taste find satisfaction in the humanized landscapes of agriculture and villages. But whatever the type of landscape, its attraction depends upon the integrity with which its particular character is expressed. This is evinced even on the smallest scale. The leaf of the *Acer saccharinum* is more beautiful than that of *Acer pseudoplatanus* because it expresses its palmate form more clearly.

In pursuance of this clarity, those who seek enjoyment of the countryside require that it shall be true countryside. The enjoyment of cities is a precious but a different thing.

Whether a scene is urban or rural depends as much upon the type of human involvement as on its extent. The definition of countryside requires that any human population which may be present is concerned mainly with the land and what grows on it, and that there is a preponderance of natural, over human, habitat. A village small and compact enough to be seen as an entity within the landscape is recognized as a country village, increasing or diminishing the quality of the scene according to its siting and architecture. It is seen as a focal point in the angle of vision. If it stretches across the angle of vision it appears as an urban area.

As in all aspects of landscape appreciation, judgement is not based solely on visual criteria. The scattered cabins of those who work the land in Connemara are accepted as natural growth from the stoney soil, but holiday bungalows along the coast are seen as urban intrusions. Men working the land, farmhouses settled into an agricultural background, are part of the rural scene, while tourists and their caravans strike a false note.

There is a more complex response to agriculture itself. When it is set within the context of natural habitats it is accepted as true countryside by all except, perhaps, by those who have known the area as wholly wild. But reaction to the degree of rigidity and extent of the man-imposed patterns, varies from one individual to another. To some the more complete and obvious the human domination the better. There is attraction in the long straight plough furrows and boundless seas of waving barley.

But to many there is a scale beyond which control becomes dull if not oppressive, however good the abstract patterns may be which it produces.

One reason for this is that scale in landscape has two criteria, the visual and the ecological. What is now known as 'ecological intuition' often causes the two to coincide.

Sight is not the only sense which responds to the landscape. If it were so, television might replace enjoyment of the outside world. But the blind

well know that contentment and exhilaration can also come through scent, sound and feeling.

Bird song, wind in the tree-tops, the snapping of seed-pods in the sun, rushing water and the utter stillness of a summer evening are as evocative as the visible world, while the scent of new mown hay or of damp mosses in the wood, may outlast the visual memory. The sheer movement of the body over the land, the sensuous enjoyment of springy turf, soft grass-heads and rustling leaves, the feel of the sun and the wind, are pleasures not to be enjoyed through the car window, but only as a participant within the landscape.

151,152
There is attraction in the clarity with which a pattern is expressed. The leaf of Acer saccharinum *is more beautiful than that of* Acer pseudoplatanus, *because it expresses its palmate form more clearly.*

153,154
Incongruous intrusions in the landscape may offend as much by their association as by their appearance. A farmhouse held within the landscape is a welcome incident, while caravans can contradict the character of countryside.

So appreciation of a landscape involves two sets of factors; the purely physical responses of sight, sound and scent, and the emotional response of association. The most evocative landscapes satisfy both criteria. The purely visual reaction responds to the composition of form and the quality of light and colour. Whether the form is dramatic or peaceful it must be true to itself; the grandeur of mountains must not be marred by a railway nor a peaceful stretch of coast by bungalows.

The shapes and colours of land and vegetation form patterns which can be appreciated just as one appreciates a work of art. The picture may be ruined by some incongruous intrusion or it may be relatively dull through lack of composition or colour. But response to a landscape is not solely visual. Memory may give the added pleasure of recollection, or of resentment at some recent change. Association plays its part; looking down from the ramparts of Troy onto the plain where the Greeks once camped, or walking along the Roman Wall in Cumbria, gives an intensity of feeling beyond that evoked by the landscape's physical features.

Greater knowledge and understanding of a landscape can intensify the enjoyment it gives. To those with long familiarity of the landscape, Interpretive Centres may even seem an intrusion, but they serve a valuable purpose in giving city dwellers greater insight and understanding of what they see. The deepest pleasure is probably experienced by those who have some special interest in the countryside – the botanists, the bird watchers and the geologists – for participation in a landscape gives a depth of feeling far beyond that enjoyed by the mere onlooker.

EPILOGUE

156,157
Scale, as well as association,
accepts a rough track as a happy
incident in the mountain scene
while a major road may disrupt
both scale and mood.

Historically there have been three stages in the relationship between men and landscape; the wild landscape untouched by man; the landscape in which men and nature co-exist; and, in great conurbations, a human monoculture. Perhaps we are now on the threshold of a new relationship.

The renaissance of the fifteenth and sixteenth centuries was motivated by men's recognition of their own humanity and by pride in their achievements. It is now time for a new renaissance in which men will recognize themselves as providing the only thinking element in the earth's ecology and will therefore accept responsibility for caring for all other species and their habitats.

If men are to succeed as the custodians of the earth, their scale of thought must range from that of the universe down to the smallest living creature. The landscape must be seen as limitless in time and unified in space, a complete body, where action in any one part will affect the whole.

The classic architectural proportions, based on the human body, must

be supplemented by the wider and more flexible proportions based on the diverse spatial needs of all species. An appreciation of the patterns of network and node, of the branching tree and the overlapping spheres of interest must modify the planners concept of rigid zones. There are no frontiers.

Just as we need to understand the ecological anatomy of the earth's surface, if we are to conserve it as a living entity, so we need to understand our visual reactions to it, if this value also is to be preserved.

What constitutes the magnificence of wide open spaces? What will or will not destroy it? A lonely signpost in the desert can accentuate its vastness, a tangle of telephone wires, destroy it. A rough track can add meaning to a remote mountain side, a full-scale road disrupt it.

A small quarry on a hillside can add distinction. At what point does it become a scar?

Since the line of transition between one type of landscape and another often forms the most distinctive and attractive scenery, the assessment of the essential boundary zone is fundamental to land planning and not always easy to define. How much of the plain is contributing to the beauty of the mountains rising from it? At what point would a structure or change of land use, detract from the sweep of a hill meeting a plain?

Such points can only be determined by the seeing eye. No hard and fast rules can replace human judgement in finding the essential element of any landscape.

To assess the value of a landscape involves a knowledge of its viability; the degree to which it fulfils its particular role as a part of the functioning surface of the earth, and, in human terms, a judgement of the visual and emotional reactions it evokes. It is impossible to assess the relative values of landscapes of different types. To some the wild is more beautiful, to others the humanized.

But it is possible to make some assessment of the value of a landscape within its own category, a judgement based largely on the integrity with which it expresses its own character and maintains its viability.

Perhaps, too, it needs the ability to identify oneself with the natural scene; an outlook which is more common in the Orient than in the Western world. A European will say "That is where I wish to plant that tree", but a Japanese may say "That is where this tree wishes to be".

Men once accepted themselves unquestioningly as part of nature. Now, after millenia of thought, invention, exploration and alienation they are ready to return full circle to take their place consciously as the one member of the ecosystem which has the knowledge and power to keep the earth both habitable for all species and still able to respond to the higher needs of an evolved human race.

158,159
A small quarry in the hillside may add interest by revealing the underlying strata, while both the form and the mood of a landscape are wrecked by large excavations.

160,161
*Zones of transition are critical
elements in the landscape. A
structure sited at the point
where hillside meets plain can
destroy the landform's flow.
The seeing eye would site it
beyond the critical zone.*

INDEX

Reference is made to concepts, themes and the photographs that illustrate them by page numbers.
Photographs are referred to in bold type.

NOTES